Printed By Createspace, An Amazon.com Company